THE UNITED STATES PRESIDENTS

## JOSEPH
# BIDEN
## OUR 46TH PRESIDENT

by Ann Gaines Rodriguez

**The Child's World®**
childsworld.com

1980 Lookout Drive • Mankato, MN 56003-1705
800-599-READ • www.childsworld.com

ISBN 9781503844377 (REINFORCED LIBRARY BINDING)
ISBN 9781503846814 (PORTABLE DOCUMENT FORMAT)
ISBN 9781503848009 (ONLINE MULTI-USER EBOOK)
LCCN 2020945266

Printed in the United States of America

# CONTENTS

*Joseph R. Biden Jr. was elected 46th president of the United States in November 2020.*

# CHAPTER ONE

# THE EARLY YEARS

Joseph Robinette Biden Jr., the 46th president of the United States, was born on November 20, 1942, in Scranton, Pennsylvania. Joe—as his family and friends call him—is the oldest of four children born to Catherine (Jean) Biden and Joseph Biden Sr. He has two brothers, Jim and Frank, and one sister, Valerie.

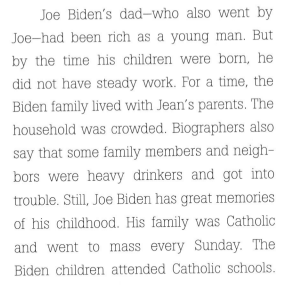

Joe Biden's dad—who also went by Joe—had been rich as a young man. But by the time his children were born, he did not have steady work. For a time, the Biden family lived with Jean's parents. The household was crowded. Biographers also say that some family members and neighbors were heavy drinkers and got into trouble. Still, Joe Biden has great memories of his childhood. His family was Catholic and went to mass every Sunday. The Biden children attended Catholic schools.

*Joe Biden was born in Scranton, Pennsylvania. From a young age, Joe loved playing sports and was a talented athlete.*

Joe's parents, Jean and Joe Sr. (pictured here in the 1980s), were loving and supportive. The Bidens were a close-knit family.

Joe was a popular boy, although quick with a punch—especially when he was teased because he stuttered. To this day Joe remembers a feeling of shame. He so feared reading out loud in class that he would look ahead in his textbook and memorize the paragraph that would be his to read. Joe practiced saying the answers to questions he expected, and he also recited poems. The family tells of a time his mother went to school in order to tell off a teacher who had made fun of young Joe's stutter.

**Joe's classmates cruelly nicknamed him "Dash" because his stuttered words sounded short and sharp, like the dashes in Morse code. They also called him "Bye-bye" because he couldn't say his full last name at times.**

In 1953, the Biden family moved from Pennsylvania to Claymont, Delaware. Joe Biden Sr. found a new job selling used cars and later managing sales at a car dealership. At first, the Biden family lived in a new apartment that wasn't fancy. A year later they rented a house. Finally, the family bought a small brick house, where Joe shared a bedroom with Jimmy, Frankie, and their uncle Ed. Joe remembers them all using one dresser with four drawers.

*Joe Biden (second from right) is the oldest of four children. When Joe was 11, the Biden family moved from Scranton to Claymont, Delaware.*

For high school, Joe enrolled at Archmere Academy, a college-preparatory school. Coming up with **tuition** was hard for his family, so Joe worked at the school every summer, doing jobs such as painting fences, washing windows, and working in the garden. While never a very good student, Joe was a sports star. He played football, and led a team that had been losing for years to an undefeated season his senior year. When Joe graduated from Archmere in 1961, he was class president.

Joe graduated from the University of Delaware in 1965 and went on to study law at Syracuse University. He and Neilia were married a year later.

**While at the University of Delaware, Joe got in trouble for playing a prank. He sprayed his dorm director (the person in charge of Joe's housing) with a fire extinguisher.**

In the fall of that year, Joe enrolled at the University of Delaware. There he studied history and **political science** and again played football. On a spring-break trip in 1964, Joe met Neilia Hunter. She was a student at Syracuse University in New York. Joe and Neilia enjoyed each other's company. They soon began dating. After Joe graduated from college in 1965, he studied law at Syracuse University.

He chose that law school because it was close to Neilia's house. Joe and Neilia married one year later, in 1966. Looking back, Joe Biden remembers that he never really got into his studies in college or law school because he was always focused on what lay ahead. Joe graduated from law school in 1968. The following year, he and Neilia started their family. They had three children together: Joseph Biden III, Robert, and Naomi.

**Joe and Neilia's three children all went by nicknames or their middle names. Joseph Biden III was called "Beau." Naomi was often called "Amy." Robert still goes by "Hunter."**

Joe (holding his sons, Beau and Hunter) and Neilia Biden (center) pose for a photo while attending a Democratic state convention in the summer of 1972.

# THE BIDEN FAMILY

By heritage, Joe Biden is mostly Irish. His mother's family came from Ireland during a potato **famine** in 1849. His father's family arrived in America around the same time. Joe's great-great grandfather was also Irish, but other ancestors were British and French.

Joe has always had a close-knit family. In his speeches, he often talks about his family and refers to things his parents said or did. Joe's mother taught her children to lean on each other. A lesson he learned from his father

is that things won't always go your way, and that's OK. "Champ, when you get knocked down, you get back up," his dad told him.

As an adult, Joe has balanced work and family life. Just as his mother wanted, he's remained close to his siblings. Joe also spends as much time as possible with his adult children and his grandchildren. The large family likes to vacation together. In the photo above, Biden is pictured with his daughter, Ashley, in 2012.

# CHAPTER TWO

# INTO POLITICS

After Joe Biden graduated from law school, he and Neilia moved to Wilmington, Delaware. He worked as a lawyer at a respected law firm, but he didn't like that kind of work. Biden became a public defender, which means he defended individuals who couldn't afford an attorney. During this time, Biden met local Democratic **politicians** who encouraged him to run for the New Castle County Council. Delaware only has three counties, so county governments play a bigger role there than in some larger states. New Castle is Delaware's largest county. Biden's family helped him **campaign,** and in 1970, he won his first elected office. Biden was just 27 years old. That year was not good for Democrats in Delaware, however. Looking back, party leaders remember that Biden's was the highest office they won that year. While serving on the council, Biden stuck up for the little guy, fighting against a proposed 10-lane highway project that would have cut into Wilmington's neighborhoods. He also called attention to oil companies' attempts to build **refineries** on Delaware's coast that would have created pollution.

**While he was a law student, Biden bought Neilia a German shepherd puppy. They named him Senator.**

The people he represented thought Biden did a good job as their coun-cilman. He received support when he decided that he wanted to move up in the political world and run for the US Senate. Every state gets two sena-tors. A man named J. Caleb Boggs held one of Delaware's Senate seats. He was a successful **Republican** politician who had been in one office or another since 1946. Boggs had served as governor, a congressman, and a senator. Biden entered the race as the underdog.

Biden and his sister, Valerie, are shown in their office during the 1970 New Castle County Council race. Valerie would help her brother win the Senate race two years later.

*Biden (pictured in 1972) was inspired to become a public defender by civil rights leaders. His desire to fight for equal rights for all Americans led him to a career in politics.*

Just as they did when Biden ran for county councilman, his family stepped up to help him. Biden's sister was his campaign manager. His brother Jimmy was in charge of fundraising. His brother Frank recruited volunteers. Neilia and Biden's mother also hosted coffees, where they talked to other Delawareans about why they should vote for Biden. In his campaign, Biden focused on four issues: the environment, taxes, crime, and the Vietnam War, which he opposed. Looking back, Biden has said that he was inspired by the **civil rights movement** to become involved in national politics.

**Biden did not have to fight in the Vietnam War. As a student, he received deferments. After graduating, a doctor disqualified Biden for service due to his asthma.**

On November 7, 1972, everyone was surprised when Joe Biden won the Senate race. Biden had beaten Boggs by just 3,000 votes. Immediately, Biden began preparing to take office. It was an exciting time for him and his family. But then tragedy struck. On December 18, 1972, Biden was in Washington, DC, getting his new office ready. Back home in Delaware, his wife and children were out shopping for a Christmas tree when they were in a terrible car accident. A huge truck hit their car. Neilia and Amy, who was just one year old, were killed in the accident. Beau and Hunter were seriously injured.

The boys were in the hospital for weeks. Although Joe Biden was overwhelmed by **grief,** he was persuaded not to give up his Senate seat.

On January 5, 1973, he was sworn into office at the hospital. His family brought Hunter, who had been released. Beau was wheeled to the ceremony with his leg in traction (a device used to help stabilize and align broken bones). Journalists were on hand to record the ceremony, which made the national news. At just 30 years old, Joe Biden was now a widower, a single father of two young boys, and a United States senator.

**With his 1972 victory, Biden became the sixth-youngest person ever elected to the US Senate.**

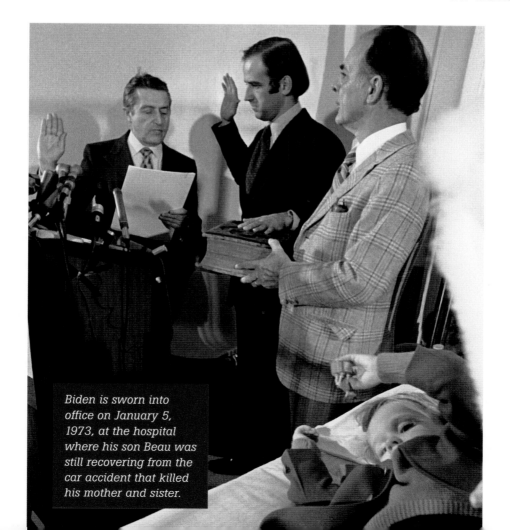

*Biden is sworn into office on January 5, 1973, at the hospital where his son Beau was still recovering from the car accident that killed his mother and sister.*

Although he made his home in Delaware, Biden's work was in Washington, DC—120 miles (193 km) away. Many senators spend weeknights in Washington, returning to their homes only on weekends or holidays. But Joe Biden **commuted** back and forth by train. His sister, Valerie, moved into his house to help take care of the boys. Biden continued to commute for years, making thousands of train trips and earning the nickname "Amtrak Joe." By commuting, Biden got to see his sons every night and every morning.

Senator Biden took the train from his home in Delaware to his office in Washington, DC, for more than 30 years.

Biden was a single parent for five years. At first, he found it difficult to focus on his new responsibilities. But over time he became interested again in government issues and policies. He started his career at a time of upheaval in American politics. Americans had pulled out of the very complicated Vietnam War. In Washington, DC, the vice president, Spiro Agnew, was accused of corruption and **resigned.** The following summer President Richard Nixon also resigned, due to the **Watergate scandal.** In a speech, Biden said he hoped Americans saw that it was the president himself, and not the Republican Party, that had done wrong. In 1974, *Time* magazine included Biden in its list of 200 Faces for the Future, calling him self-confident and ambitious.

In 1975, Biden's family started a new chapter in their lives. Joe met Jill Jacobs, a high school English teacher. Joe and Jill soon fell in love. Beau and Hunter liked her very much, too. In 1977, the couple was married at the United Nations Chapel in New York City. Four years later, a daughter named Ashley was born.

**Joe Biden took the Amtrak train for more than 30 years. He got to know the train crews so well, he sometimes called them his family. He even hosted parties and cookouts for some of the crew members at his home.**

Joe met Jill Jacobs in 1975, and they got married two years later. Joe said that falling in love with Jill "made me start to think my family might be whole again."

**During his time as a senator, Biden was one of the poorest people in Congress. Many other senators and representatives had investments or came from wealthy families. Biden never made much more than his Senate salary.**

By that time, Biden was nearing the end of his first term as senator. He went on to be reelected six times, holding office under seven presidents. In the Senate, Biden gained a reputation as a **moderate,** and as someone who could see things from a working person's point of view. Over the years, he formed friendships with many other senators, both Democrats and Republicans. But Biden did become known for talking a great deal—sometimes too much—and sometimes putting his foot in his mouth.

Biden came to hold important positions in the Senate throughout his career. In 1981, he became the **ranking minority member** of the Senate's Judiciary Committee. This committee oversees the Department of Justice and the FBI. It holds hearings when the president nominates someone to federal courts, including the Supreme Court. In 1987, Biden served as chair, or leader, of the committee. He held the position for eight years.

Joe Biden speaks during a hearing of the Senate Judiciary Committee in 1987.

Mr. THURMOND

Mr. BIDEN

Biden served on the Senate Foreign Relations committee for many years, and he has been its chairperson, too. That committee works with the nation's **allies,** overseeing foreign-aid funding and arms sales. Doing that work, Biden talked to many world leaders.

Senator Biden wrote and sponsored bills, including many that became laws. And, like many other members of Congress and the Senate, Biden worked to further the interests of his home state. In 1999, he achieved a milestone, casting his 10,000th vote.

*Senator Biden talks to reporters after a press conference regarding matters of the Senate Foreign Relations committee.*

Biden and his family wave to supporters at the Wilmington train station after announcing his run in the presidential election in 1987.

It was while he was a senator that Joe Biden first contemplated running for president of the United States. In 1987, he threw his hat into the ring for the first time, announcing himself as a presidential **candidate** at the Wilmington train station on June 9. He seemed likely to appeal to many, because of his moderate stance. A likeable man, Biden had an ability to listen and connect well with people. He also had a good campaign manager—his sister, Valerie. She became the first woman to manage both Senate and presidential campaigns.

However, Biden's campaign ran into trouble. Newspapers reported that in some speeches, Biden used the words of others without giving them proper credit. Then it was revealed that Biden had done the same in a law school paper years before. He was also accused of lying about how well he did at school. On September 23, Biden withdrew from the race.

In February 1988, Biden suffered an **aneurysm.** He needed brain surgery. He suffered another aneurysm three months later. These health scares caused Biden to think hard about what he wanted in life. He said after that, "I no longer felt I had to win *every* moment to succeed."

In 2007, Joe Biden again declared his candidacy for US president. At that point, President George W. Bush had been president for eight years. Americans were very concerned about the economy and a war in Iraq. Biden felt he understood the serious issues facing the nation—and had the experience necessary to lead.

Biden, chairman of the Senate Foreign Relations Committee, prepares for a hearing on Capitol Hill to discuss the war in Iraq.

# DELAWARE

Delaware is an eastern state, surrounded by Pennsylvania, Maryland, New Jersey, and the Atlantic Ocean. Delaware is the second-smallest state—just 96 miles (154 km) long and 35 miles (56 km) wide. In terms of population, it's 45th in size, with around one million residents. Delaware has a high population together. Delaware was one of the original 13 colonies and prides itself on being the first state to ratify the Constitution. Joe Biden is Delaware's longest-serving senator. Biden's son Beau was the attorney general of Delaware from 2007 to 2015. Today the Bidens are recognized as Delaware's most famous family.

# CHAPTER THREE

# VICE PRESIDENT

Americans decide who will be their political party's presidential nominee through presidential **caucuses** and **primary** elections. In 2008, the first election for the Democrats was held in Iowa. Candidates Barack Obama, John Edwards, and Hillary Clinton all won **delegates** to the Democratic convention. Joe Biden did not win many votes, and he dropped out of the race.

Biden remained in the news, however. By June, Barack Obama had won enough delegates to become the Democratic nominee. Still in his forties and having served just one term in the Senate, Obama did not have a lot of political experience at the time. He needed a running mate who could appeal to **blue-collar workers.** Obama was looking for a vice president who would help him with **foreign policy** and national security. In fact, Obama told an aide he wanted someone with gray hair.

*Joe Biden greets supporters during his run for the presidency in 2007.*

Earlier, Joe Biden had not made a good impression on Obama. They had served on a committee together in the Senate, and Biden had invited Obama to dinner. He said he would pick up the bill. Biden remembered Obama's reply—that he could afford to pay. In addition, some people thought Biden might be racist when Obama entered the presidential campaign because he'd described Obama as being "clean." Although Biden had meant that Obama was fresh and new to the campaign scene, he felt badly that his comment was confusing. He called Obama to apologize, and Obama said it wasn't necessary. Biden was always respectful to him on the debate stage.

Joe Biden hugs Barack Obama at the Democratic National Convention. Biden had just formally accepted his nomination as the Democratic vice-presidential candidate.

Because of Biden's experience, Obama decided that Biden should hold a position in his **administration.** There was talk of him as **Secretary of State,** the president's chief foreign affairs adviser. But then on August 23, the Obama campaign announced that Joe Biden was his pick as vice president. The two held their first **rally** that day and appeared together at the Democratic National Convention in Denver just a few days later. In the months that followed, the Obama and Biden families spent time together on the road. They got along well, and eventually became fast friends. Biden did not attract as much news coverage as the Republican vice presidential candidate, Sarah Palin, the governor of Alaska. Still, the public considered Biden the winner when the two met on the debate stage.

**Although they disagreed on several issues, Biden and President Obama became good friends during their years together, and they're still friends today. President Obama has even referred to Biden as "my brother."**

On November 4, 2008, Obama and Biden won their race—with 53 percent of the vote. They also won in the **Electoral College.** Joe Biden won reelection to the Senate, too—he hadn't dropped out of that race in case he wasn't elected vice president. On January 20, 2009, Obama and Biden were sworn into office. The Bidens moved into the vice president's house at the Naval Observatory. This was the first time they'd lived in Washington, DC, and the first time Joe didn't have to commute to work. One thing he especially liked about the house was its pool. Biden's wife, Jill, loved exploring the grounds. Their grandchildren often came for sleepovers. The Bidens also hosted parties and held meetings in the house's formal rooms.

Biden is sworn in as vice president on January 20, 2009, at the US Capitol in Washington, DC. His wife, Jill, and family members stand beside him as he takes the oath of office.

In the course of American history, vice presidents have sometimes been seen as unimportant. Some presidents do not give their vice presidents much to do. But over time, President Obama assigned Biden important responsibilities both in their first term and after they were reelected in 2012. Vice President Biden helped pass, and then implement, the Recovery Act, which enabled the United States to get out of a serious economic **recession.** He worked for the passage of the Affordable Care Act, helped organize the government's response to the Ebola virus, promoted women's rights and equality, and pushed for the government to address climate change.

**The Affordable Care Act (ACA) is sometimes called "Obamacare." People have argued over it for years. Supporters of the ACA say it makes health insurance available to more people, and it lowers medical costs. Critics feel the ACA raises costs in other areas and causes taxes to increase.**

In the area of foreign relations, Biden worked toward peace in troubled parts of the world, including Korea, Iraq, and the **Ukraine.** As vice president, he spoke to other world leaders regularly and often in person, traveling 1.2 million miles (1.9 million km) to more than 50 countries. Biden once recalled how much he enjoyed it when he could take a grandchild along on a trip.

Looking back, Joe Biden remembers enjoying his vice presidency, both because of his accomplishments and what came to be a deep friendship with Barack Obama. But it was also a time of sadness for the Biden family.

*President Obama awarded Biden the Presidential Medal of Freedom with Distinction in 2017, calling Biden "the best vice president America's ever had."*

Beau Biden, Joe's oldest son, was diagnosed with brain cancer in 2013. He underwent surgery and medical treatments to keep the disease under control. For months, Joe Biden found himself dividing his time between his work and his family. Beau died from cancer on May 30, 2015.

Biden was heartbroken by the loss of his son. But Beau's illness and death caused Joe to think long and hard about running for president in 2016. President Obama's second term was coming to an end. Biden believed that he was qualified to lead the nation. Hillary Clinton, who had served as Obama's Secretary of State, came to Biden's house to tell him that she was going to run for the presidency in 2016. Biden decided that he didn't have time to plan an effective campaign. He decided it was time to enjoy life as a private citizen.

**At the very end of their term, Obama surprised Joe Biden by awarding him the Presidential Medal of Freedom with Distinction—the highest civilian honor there is.**

# JILL JACOBS BIDEN

Dr. Jill Biden was born Jill Tracy Jacobs in 1951. She grew up in Pennsylvania. In 1970, Jill married Bill Stevenson. She was not quite 19, and had just started college. The young couple drifted apart, and by 1974 they had separated.

Jill decided to change schools. She enrolled at the University of Delaware, and soon made new friends. She met Frank Biden, who thought Jill and his brother Joe would make a good pair. Frank set the two up on a date in 1975. He was right—Jill and Joe liked each other right away. The couple soon began seeing much more of each other.

As Jill and Joe dated, she got to know Beau and Hunter. The boys liked Jill so much, they encouraged their father to marry her. In 1977, Jill and Joe got married in New York City. In 1981, they had a daughter named Ashley.

Jill worked as a teacher and continued studying education. She earned a master's degree in education in 1981, and a second master's degree in 1987. In 2007, Jill earned a doctoral degree in educational leadership. She continued to teach, even throughout the fall of 2008 while she was campaigning for her husband and Barack Obama. Dr. Biden even graded papers on the campaign bus!

As Second Lady, Dr. Biden continued to work, teaching at North Virginia Community College. At the same time, she worked on a variety of initiatives to help all Americans. She raised awareness of the value of community colleges. She also showcased the needs of American military families.

Dr. Biden is also an author. In 2012, she published *Don't Forget, God Bless Our Troops*. This children's book tells the story of a young girl whose father has gone to war. After her husband left office, Dr. Biden wrote a **memoir** titled *Where the Light Enters*. In 2020, she wrote another children's book called *Joey*. It tells the story of Joe Biden as a child.

# CHAPTER FOUR

# EYES ON THE PRIZE

After Donald Trump was **inaugurated** as the 45th US president on January 20, 2017, the Bidens once again took the train home to Wilmington, Delaware. For the first time in 45 years, Joe Biden held no political office. He and his wife started a foundation, and he wrote an autobiography, *Promise Me, Dad*, which told the story of the year Beau died. Soon, the former vice president would establish **think tanks** at two universities: the Biden Institute at the University of Delaware, and the Penn Biden Center for Diplomacy & Engagement at the University of Pennsylvania. Biden enjoyed spending time with his family and working on projects he considered important. However, he could not help but feel that the nation was in trouble. On April 25, 2019, Biden announced that he was running for president for the third time. In his video announcing his candidacy, he criticized President Trump.

Biden takes a selfie with a student at Rutgers University after giving a speech there. In 2019, the former vice president announced his candidacy in the 2020 presidential election.

At that point, Joe Biden was 76 years old. That made him one of the oldest people ever to run for president. As a moderate with a long political career behind him, Biden had experience. But he faced challenges. Many Democrats wondered whether Biden was **progressive** enough to appeal to young voters. Also, he received criticism for decisions he made, opinions he had held, and bills he had sponsored years earlier. However, Biden has openly discussed changes to his own thinking, and he has taken responsibility for what he now sees as mistakes.

*Today, Biden recognizes past decisions or old views that he now sees as mistakes, such as the way in which Anita Hill was treated during the judiciary hearings Biden led in 1991 (pictured).*

Democratic presidential candidates (including Biden, sixth from left) pose together for a photo before their debate in October 2019. It was the most diverse group of candidates in US history.

For example, in 1991 Biden was chairman of the Senate Judiciary Committee. A woman named Anita Hill accused US Supreme Court nominee Clarence Thomas of sexual harassment. It was Biden's job to lead the hearings. He has said that he now regrets the way in which Hill was treated.

From the beginning of the 2020 presidential race, Biden was seen as a **front-runner.** But many other strong Democratic candidates were also in the race. In fact, in June 2019, the party had to hold two nights of debates in order to accommodate 20 candidates. It was also the most diverse field, including six women, two African American senators, a Hispanic former **cabinet** member, the first openly gay candidate, and the first Asian American candidate.

*Biden speaks at a campaign rally in South Carolina in February 2020.*

As time went by, candidates began dropping out of the race. Presidential political campaigns are very expensive, and some candidates had trouble raising enough money. Others couldn't gain enough public support. Early in 2020, the Democratic Party began to hold presidential primaries and caucuses. The first was in February in Iowa, and Biden came in fourth. But as the weeks went by, he did better, and his campaign gained momentum. On **Super Tuesday,** Biden won 10 of 14 states.

But the world was about to change in a massive way. In late 2019, a **coronavirus** had begun spreading across the world. It caused a deadly lung disease called COVID-19. It spread through droplets in the air that people breathed in through their nose or mouth.

By 2020, millions of people were infected in a global **pandemic.** People were dying at an alarming rate. Countries shut down in hopes of keeping the illness from spreading. Restaurants, stores, businesses, churches, and schools closed. Airports were almost entirely empty. Large gatherings such as concerts were canceled. People stayed in their homes to keep healthy and safe. Meetings and classes were held **virtually** on computers. If anyone needed to go to public places, they were urged to wear a mask over their nose and mouth.

COVID-19 stands for "coronavirus disease 2019." The year 2019 is when the disease was discovered. By the end of 2020, COVID-19 had sickened more than 65 million people worldwide. More than 1.5 million of those people died, and more than 275,000 of those deaths were Americans.

*People crossing the Brooklyn Bridge in New York City wear masks to help prevent the spread of COVID-19. By November 2020, more than 30,000 New Yorkers had died from the virus.*

The Bidens wave to supporters after Joe Biden gave his first speech as president-elect. "I pledge to be a president who seeks not to divide, but to unify," he said. "Who doesn't see Red and Blue states, but a United States. And who will work with all my heart to win the confidence of the whole people."

With so many businesses closing, economies around the world suffered. Many Americans lost their jobs or had to take pay cuts. People were unhappy with the way the current president, Donald Trump, had handled the pandemic. They felt it was time for a change in leadership. Joe Biden had a plan to get the United States back on track. He campaigned virtually and explained to citizens how he could help lead the county out of the crisis. Many Americans liked Biden's ideas. They liked his empathy for the people who had been sickened or who had died from the disease. Most importantly, they liked Biden's experience, strength, and leadership skills.

November 3 was Election Day. Voters were bitterly divided on many issues, including the pandemic. Americans voted in record numbers, and in some states a clear winner couldn't be decided right away. Many people had voted by mail in order to stay safe during the pandemic. It took several days for all of the votes to be counted. On November 7, it was finally announced that Joe Biden had been elected 46th president of the United States. In a speech that night, Biden called for Americans to be united once again. He closed his speech with these words:

**The 2020 election had the highest voter turnout in modern American history. Biden received more than 80 million votes.**

"[L]et us be the nation that we know we can be—a nation united, a nation strengthened, a nation healed, the United States of America."

# KAMALA HARRIS

Kamala Devi Harris was born in Oakland, California, in 1964. Her parents were both immigrants. Kamala's mother was born in India, and her father was born in Jamaica. Kamala's parents divorced when she and her sister, Maya, were little. Raised by their single mother, the girls lived in Berkeley, California.

The family moved to Montreal in Quebec, Canada, when Kamala was 12. She returned to the United States to attend college at Howard University in Washington, DC. While there, Kamala became interested in debating. She graduated with a degree in political science and economics in 1981.

Harris went on to become a lawyer. In 1990, she began working in the district attorney's office in Alameda County, California. Her job was to prove cases against people accused of a crime. In 2003, she was elected district attorney for the City and County of San Francisco. She was then elected attorney general of California in 2011. An attorney general is the top legal officer in a state. California's attorney general office is the largest in the nation.

In 2016, Harris won election to the US Senate. As a senator, Harris served on important committees, including the Senate Judiciary Committee. She fought for fair wages, justice system reform, expansion of health care, and help for people struggling with addictions.

In January 2019, Harris announced she was running for president of the United States. Harris dropped out of the race that December, but she supported Joe Biden as he continued his campaign. On August 11, 2020, Biden named Harris as his choice for vice president.

After she and Biden won the election in November 2020, Kamala Harris became the first woman, and the first Indian American and African American, to ever be elected vice president of the United States. In a speech to a cheering crowd, Harris said, "While I may be the first woman in this office, I will not be the last."

# TIME LINE

| 1940 | 1950 | 1960 | 1970 | 1980–1990 |
|------|------|------|------|-----------|

**1942**
Joseph Robinette Biden Jr. is born on November 20 in Scranton, Pennsylvania, to Catherine Eugenia "Jean" Finnegan and Joseph R. Biden Sr.

**1953**
The Biden family moves from Pennsylvania to Claymont, Delaware.

**1966**
Joe Biden and Neilia Hunter marry. They would have three children: Beau, Hunter, and Naomi.

**1970**
Biden wins his first elected office, serving on the New Castle County Council in Delaware.

**1972**
Biden, 29 years old, wins his election to the Senate on November 7. On December 18, his wife, Neilia, and baby daughter are killed in a car accident. Beau and Hunter survive the accident but are seriously injured.

**1973**
On January 5, Biden is sworn in as a US senator of Delaware at his son Beau's hospital bedside.

**1977**
Joe Biden marries schoolteacher Jill Jacobs; four years later, their daughter, Ashley, is born.

**1981**
Biden becomes the ranking minority member of the Senate's Judiciary Committee.

**1987**
Biden enters the presidential race for the 1988 election but withdraws three months later.

**1988**
Biden undergoes brain surgery to repair an aneurysm.

**1990**
In January, Biden introduces a bill that becomes the Violence Against Women Act, which addresses sexual assault and domestic violence. President Clinton signs the bill into law in 1994.

### 2007

Biden enters the presidential race for the second time but withdraws. He is elected chairman of the Senate Foreign Relations Committee. His memoir, *Promises to Keep*, is published in August.

### 2008

On August 23, Biden is named the vice presidential running mate of Barack Obama. On November 4, Obama and Biden win the election.

### 2009

On January 20, Biden is sworn in as vice president of the United States. Obama becomes the nation's first African American president. Biden oversees the implementation of the Recovery Act.

### 2012

President Obama and Vice President Biden are reelected on November 6.

### 2015

Biden's son Beau dies from brain cancer at age 46 on May 30. In October, Biden announces that he won't run in the 2016 presidential election.

### 2017

On January 12, President Obama awards Biden the Presidential Medal of Freedom, the nation's highest civilian honor. In February, Joe and Jill Biden establish the Biden Foundation. Biden's book *Promise Me, Dad* is published in November.

### 2019

On April 25, Biden announces his candidacy for US president in the 2020 election. Dr. Jill Biden publishes her memoir, *Where the Light Enters*, in May. In December, the first cases of what would later be identified as a novel coronavirus (eventually named COVID-19 by the World Health Organization) are reported in Wuhan, China.

### 2020

In March, the World Health Organization declares the coronavirus outbreak a pandemic. Much of the United States goes into lockdown. On August 11, Biden names California senator Kamala Harris as his running mate. Biden accepts his party's nomination as the Democratic presidential candidate in a speech during the mostly virtual Democratic National Convention on August 20. On November 7, four days after Election Day, Biden and Harris win the election against President Donald Trump and Vice President Mike Pence.

**administration** (ad-min-STRAY-shun): An administration is made up of people who work in the executive branch of government during a president's time in office. Obama knew that Biden would be a good addition to his administration because of Biden's experience.

**allies** (AL-lize): Allies are nations that provide assistance and support to each other. While serving on the Senate Foreign Relations committee, Biden often worked with America's allies.

**aneurysm** (AN-yuh-ri-zem): An aneurysm is a blood-filled bulge of a blood vessel. It's often in an artery of the brain or heart. Biden underwent brain surgery in 1988 to repair an aneurysm.

**attorney general** (uh-TUR-nee JEN-rul): An attorney general is the chief lawyer of a country or state who represents the government in legal matters. Beau Biden was the attorney general of Delaware.

**blue-collar workers** (BLOO-KA-ler WUR-kers): Blue-collar workers refer to people who have jobs that require physical labor, such as construction or manufacturing work. Barack Obama believed that Biden could help him gain support from blue-collar workers.

**cabinet** (KAB-nit): A cabinet is the group of people who advise a president. One of the Democratic presidential candidates that Biden debated against was a member of President Obama's cabinet.

**campaign** (kam-PAYN): A campaign is the process of running for an election, including activities such as giving speeches or attending rallies. Biden's family helped him campaign for his first elected office.

**candidate** (KAN-duh-dayt): A candidate is a person who is running in an election. At least two candidates run for president every four years.

**caucuses** (KAW-kus-ez): Members of a political party have a caucus, or meeting, to choose presidential nominees for their party. Biden didn't receive a lot of support from caucuses in 2008, so he dropped out of the race.

**civil rights movement** (SIV-el RYTZ MOOV-ment): The civil rights movement was the struggle for equal rights for African Americans in the United States during the 1950s and 1960s. Biden became involved in politics because he was inspired by the civil rights movement.

**commuted** (kuh-MYOO-ted): To commute means to travel back and forth regularly. Although Biden lived in Delaware, he commuted to Washington every day when he was a senator.

**convention** (kun-VEN-shun): A convention is a meeting. The political parties each hold a national convention every four years to choose a presidential candidate.

**coronavirus** (kuh-ROH-nuh-vy-rus): The coronavirus is a virus that's spread through droplets in the air. It can damage a person's lungs and airways. Many people wear masks covering their mouth and nose to avoid spreading the potentially deadly disease.

**deferments** (dih-FUR-munts): A deferment is the act of delaying or postponing something. When Biden was in college, he received deferments that allowed him to avoid serving in the military during the Vietnam War.

**delegates** (DEL-uh-gets): Delegates are representatives who are chosen or elected to vote or act for others. Biden dropped out of the presidential race in 2008 because he didn't have delegate support.

**Democratic** (dem-uh-KRAT-ik): If something is Democratic, it is related to the Democratic Party. Biden was the Democratic presidential nominee in the 2020 election.

**Electoral College** (ee-LEKT-uh-rul KOL-ij): The Electoral College is made up of representatives from each state who vote for candidates in presidential elections. Members of the Electoral College cast their votes based on which candidate most people in their state prefer.

**famine** (FAM-un): A famine is a widespread and extreme lack of food. More than a million people died in the famine in Ireland from 1845 to 1852.

**foreign policy** (FOR-un PAWL-uh-see): A foreign policy is the strategies and plans a country holds to achieve its own goals or protect its national interests in dealing with other nations. Barack Obama appreciated Biden's experience and knowledge of foreign policy and national security.

**front-runner** (FRUNT RUH-ner): The front-runner is the person most likely to win a race or competition. Some considered Biden as the front-runner during the 2020 election.

**grief** (GREEF): Grief is feeling deep sadness caused especially by someone's death. Biden was overwhelmed by grief when his first wife and daughter were killed in a car accident.

**inaugurated** (ih-NAWG-yuh-ray-ted): To be inaugurated is to be sworn into office in a ceremony, as when a president begins a new term. US presidents are inaugurated on January 20.

**memoir** (MEM-wahr): A memoir is a written account of someone's personal experience. Dr. Biden published her memoir in 2019.

**moderate** (MA-duh-rut): In politics, a moderate is someone who expresses political beliefs that are neither very liberal nor very conservative. Biden could appeal to voters from opposing political parties because of his moderate stance.

**pandemic** (pan-DEM-ik): A pandemic is a disease that occurs over a wide geographic area and affects a high proportion of the population. The coronavirus pandemic greatly impacted campaigning and conventions during the 2020 election.

**political science** (puh-LIT-uh-kul SYE-unss): Political science is the study of government and politics. Biden studied political science at the University of Delaware.

**politicians** (pawl-uh-TISH-unz): Politicians are men and women who hold an office in government. Biden became interested in running for city council in Delaware after talking to local politicians.

**primary** (PRY-mayr-ee): A primary is an election in which people of the same political party run against each other for the chance to become their party's candidate. Biden didn't win the primary election in 2008 and soon dropped out of the presidential race.

**progressive** (pru-GREH-siv): Someone who advocates for social reform and supports advancements in science, technology, and economic development to improve society is considered progressive. Many Democrats worried if Biden's views were progressive enough to gain support from young voters.

**rally** (RA-lee): A rally is a public gathering or meeting to support or oppose someone or something. Biden and Obama held many rallies while campaigning during the 2008 election.

**ranking minority member** (RANK-ing muh-NOR-uh-tee MEM-bur): The most senior member representing the minority party is the ranking minority member of the committee. Biden was the ranking minority member of the Senate's Judiciary Committee in 1981.

**ratify** (RA-tuh-fy): To ratify something is to formally approve or confirm it. Delaware was the first state to ratify the US Constitution in 1787.

**recession** (rih-SESH-uhn): A recession is a period of time when the economy slows. The US economy was in a recession during President Obama's first term in office.

**refineries** (rih-FY-nuh-reez): A refinery is a facility where raw materials are converted into valuable substances, such as crude oil made into gasoline. Biden fought against building oil refineries in Delaware that would cause pollution.

**Republican** (rih-PUB-li-kun): A Republican is someone who is a member of the Republican political party. Biden beat his Republican opponent in the 1972 Senate race.

**resigned** (ree-ZINED): A person who resigned from a job gave it up. President Richard Nixon and Vice President Spiro Agnew both resigned from office.

**Secretary of State** (SE-kruh-tayr-ee uv STAYT): The Secretary of State is the chief adviser to the president on foreign affairs. Hillary Clinton served as President Obama's Secretary of State from 2009 to 2013.

**Super Tuesday** (SOO-pur TOOZ-day): The Tuesday in February or March of a presidential election year when the majority of US states hold primary elections to select delegates for each party's presidential candidates.

**think tanks** (THINK TANKZ): A think tank is an organization that helps solve problems for other organizations or groups by doing research and providing information, ideas, and advice. After serving as vice president, Biden founded two think tanks.

**tuition** (too-WIH-shun): Tuition is the price or payment of instruction. When he was in high school, Biden worked every summer to help pay for his tuition.

**Ukraine** (yoo-KRAYN): Ukraine is a country in eastern Europe. It was part of the Soviet Union from 1922 to 1991.

**virtually** (VER-choo-wuh-lee): When something is virtual, it occurs or exists primarily online. During the coronavirus pandemic, schools were closed, and students attended classes virtually from their homes.

**Watergate scandal** (WAH-ter-gayt SKAN-dul): A scandal is a shameful action that shocks the public. The Watergate scandal involved President Nixon. Nixon was tied to a crime in which former government agents broke into the offices of the Democratic National Committee's headquarters in order to spy on Nixon's political rivals. Nixon resigned from office due to the scandal.

# THE UNITED STATES GOVERNMENT

The United States government is divided into three equal branches: the executive, the legislative, and the judicial. This division helps prevent abuses of power because each branch has to answer to the other two. No one branch can become too powerful.

## EXECUTIVE BRANCH

President
Vice President
Departments

The job of the executive branch is to enforce the laws. It is headed by the president, who serves as the spokesperson for the United States around the world. The president has the power to sign bills into law. He or she also appoints important officials, such as federal judges, who are then confirmed by the US Senate. The president is also the commander in chief of the US military. He or she is assisted by the vice president, who takes over if the president dies or cannot carry out the duties of the office.

The executive branch also includes various departments, each focused on a specific topic. They include the Defense Department, the Justice Department, and the Agriculture Department. The department heads, along with other officials such as the vice president, serve as the president's closest advisers, called the cabinet.

## LEGISLATIVE BRANCH

Congress: Senate and the
House of Representatives

The job of the legislative branch is to make the laws. It consists of Congress, which is divided into two parts: the Senate and the House of Representatives. The Senate has 100 members, and the House of Representatives has 435 members. Each state has two senators. The number of representatives a state has varies depending on the state's population.

Besides making laws, Congress also passes budgets and enacts taxes. In addition, it is responsible for declaring war, maintaining the military, and regulating trade with other countries.

## JUDICIAL BRANCH

Supreme Court
Courts of Appeals
District Courts

The job of the judicial branch is to interpret the laws. It consists of the nation's federal courts. Trials are held in district courts. During trials, judges must decide what laws mean and how they apply. Courts of appeals review the decisions made in district courts.

The nation's highest court is the Supreme Court. If someone disagrees with a court of appeals ruling, he or she can ask the Supreme Court to review it. The Supreme Court may refuse. The Supreme Court makes sure that decisions and laws do not violate the Constitution.

# CHOOSING THE PRESIDENT

It may seem odd, but American voters don't elect the president directly. Instead, the president is chosen using what is called the Electoral College.

Each state gets as many votes in the Electoral College as its combined total of senators and representatives in Congress. For example, Iowa has two senators and four representatives, so it gets six electoral votes. Although the District of Columbia does not have any voting members in Congress, it gets three electoral votes. Usually, the candidate who wins the most votes in any given state receives all of that state's electoral votes.

To become president, a candidate must get more than half of the Electoral College votes. There are a total of 538 votes in the Electoral College, so a candidate needs 270 votes to win. If nobody receives 270 Electoral College votes, the House of Representatives chooses the president.

With the Electoral College system, the person who receives the most votes nationwide does not always receive the most electoral votes. This happened most recently in 2016, when Hillary Clinton received nearly 2.9 million more national votes than Donald J. Trump. Trump became president because he had more Electoral College votes.

The White House is the official home of the president of the United States. It is located at 1600 Pennsylvania Avenue NW in Washington, DC. In 1792, a contest was held to select the architect who would design the president's home. James Hoban won. Construction took eight years.

The first president, George Washington, never lived in the White House. The second president, John Adams, moved into the house in 1800, though the inside was not yet complete. During the War of 1812, British soldiers burned down much of the White House. It was rebuilt several years later.

The White House was changed through the years. Porches were added, and President Theodore Roosevelt added the West Wing. President William Taft changed the shape of the presidential office, making it into the famous Oval Office. While Harry Truman was president, the old house was discovered to be structurally weak. All the walls were reinforced with steel, and the rooms were rebuilt.

Today, the White House has 132 rooms (including 35 bathrooms), 28 fireplaces, and 3 elevators. It takes 570 gallons of paint to cover the outside of the six-story building. The White House provides the president with many ways to relax. It includes a putting green, a jogging track, a swimming pool, a basketball and tennis court, and beautifully landscaped gardens. The White House also has a movie theater, a billiard room, and a one-lane bowling alley.

# PRESIDENTIAL PERKS

The job of president of the United States is challenging. It is probably one of the most stressful jobs in the world. Because of this, presidents are paid well, though not nearly as well as the leaders of large corporations. In 2020, the president earned $400,000 a year. Presidents also receive extra benefits that make the demanding job a little more appealing.

★ **Camp David:** In the 1940s, President Franklin D. Roosevelt chose this heavily wooded spot in the mountains of Maryland to be the presidential retreat, where presidents can relax. Even though it is a retreat, world business is conducted there. Most famously, President Jimmy Carter met with Middle Eastern leaders at Camp David in 1978. The result was a peace agreement between Israel and Egypt.

★ ***Air Force One:*** The president flies on a jet called *Air Force One*. It is a Boeing 747-200B that has been modified to meet the president's needs. *Air Force One* is the size of a large home. It is equipped with a dining room, sleeping quarters, a conference room, and office space. It also has two kitchens that can provide food for up to 100 people.

★ **The Secret Service:** While not the most glamorous of the president's perks, the Secret Service is one of the most important. The Secret Service is a group of highly trained agents who protect the president and the president's family.

★ **The Presidential State Car:** The presidential state car is a customized Cadillac limousine. It has been armored to protect the president in case of attack. Inside the plush car are a foldaway desk, an entertainment center, and a communications console.

★ **The Food:** The White House has five chefs who will make any food the president wants. The White House also has an extensive wine collection and vegetable and fruit gardens.

★ **Retirement:** A former president receives a pension, or retirement pay, of just under $208,000 a year. Former presidents also receive health care coverage and Secret Service protection for the rest of their lives.

## QUALIFICATIONS

To run for president, a candidate must
- ★ be at least 35 years old
- ★ be a citizen who was born in the United States
- ★ have lived in the United States for 14 years

## TERM OF OFFICE

A president's term of office is four years. No president can stay in office for more than two terms.

## ELECTION DATE

The presidential election takes place every four years on the first Tuesday after November 1.

## INAUGURATION DATE

Presidents are inaugurated on January 20.

## OATH OF OFFICE

I do solemnly swear I will faithfully execute the office of the President of the United States and will to the best of my ability preserve, protect, and defend the Constitution of the United States.

## WRITE A LETTER TO THE PRESIDENT

One of the best things about being a US citizen is that Americans get to participate in their government. They can speak out if they feel government leaders aren't doing their jobs. They can also praise leaders who are going the extra mile. Do you have something you'd like the president to do? Should the president worry more about the environment and the effects of climate change? Should the government spend more money on our schools? You can write a letter to the president to say how you feel!

> 1600 Pennsylvania Avenue NW
> Washington, DC 20500

You can even write a message to the president at **whitehouse.gov/contact**.

# FOR MORE INFORMATION

## BOOKS

Beckett, Leslie. *Does Voting Matter?*
New York, NY: KidHaven, 2018.

Biden, Jill. *Joey: The Story of Joe Biden.*
New York, NY: Simon & Schuster Books for Young Readers, 2020.

Croy, Anita. *Presidential Power: How Far Does Executive Power Go?* New York, NY: Lucent, 2020.

Gormley, Beatrice. *Joe Biden: A Biography for Young Readers.*
New York, NY: Aladdin, 2021.

Grimes, Nikki. *Kamala Harris: Rooted in Justice.*
New York, NY: Atheneum Books for Young Readers, 2020.

Latta, Sara. *What Is COVID-19?*
Mankato, MN: The Child's World, 2021.

Rubinstein, Justine. *The Senate.*
Philadelphia, PA: Mason Crest, 2019.

## INTERNET SITES

Visit our website for lots of links about
Joseph Biden and other US presidents:

**childsworld.com/links**

*Note to Parents, Teachers, and Librarians: We routinely verify our web links to make sure they are safe, active sites. Encourage your readers to check them out!*